5 STEPS TO DRAWING
MAGICAL CREATURES

by Amanda StJohn • illustrated by Laura Ferraro Close

The Child's World®

Published by The Child's World®
1980 Lookout Drive • Mankato, MN 56003-1705
800-599-READ • www.childsworld.com

ACKNOWLEDGMENTS
The Child's World®: Mary Berendes, Publishing Director
The Design Lab: Design and production
Red Line Editorial: Editorial direction

ISBN: 978-1-60973-198-4
LCCN: 2011927707

Printed in the United States of America
Mankato, MN
July 2011
PA02088

TABLE OF CONTENTS

STORIES OF MAGICAL CREATURES

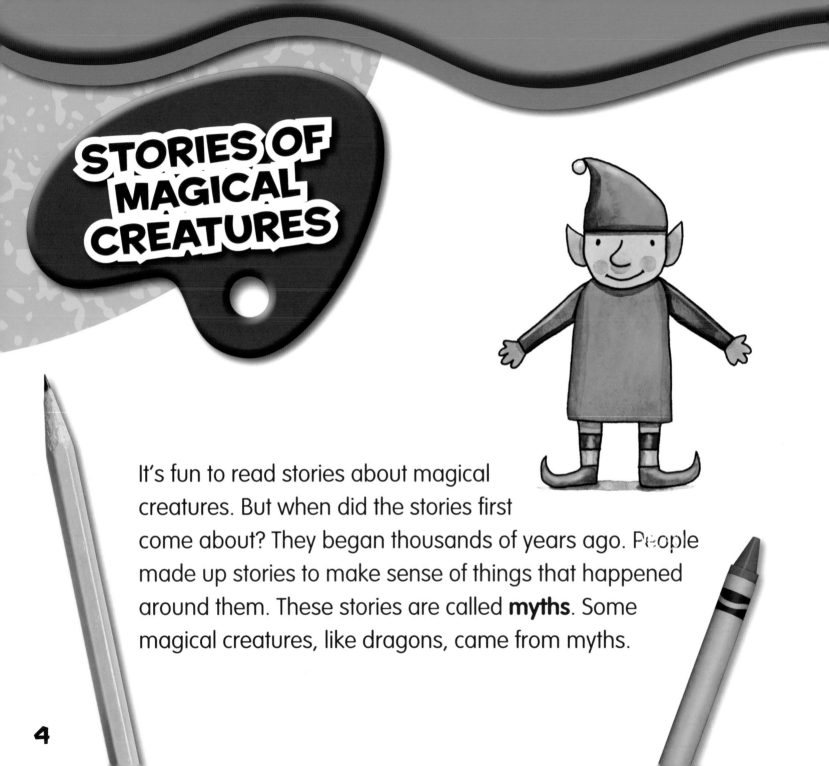

It's fun to read stories about magical creatures. But when did the stories first come about? They began thousands of years ago. People made up stories to make sense of things that happened around them. These stories are called **myths**. Some magical creatures, like dragons, came from myths.

Other magical creatures are from **folklore**. Folklore is the beliefs and customs of a group of people. Folklore about magical creatures became stories. Then the stories were passed down from family to family.

Fairies are part of folklore from Europe. Some people say fairies began as people who lived in Ireland. The people fled into the woods to escape their enemies. They blended more and more with nature. Then they turned into fairies. This is why most fairies like to hide from humans and live in forests.

FEATURES OF MAGICAL CREATURES

Magical creatures come in different forms. They can look like humans, animals, or a mixture of the two. Fairies, gnomes, and leprechauns look like humans. They are called "wee folk" because they look like short or small people. Wee folk live in communities, just like humans do.

Dragons and unicorns are magical animals. Dragons are scary beasts. They have thick scales and sharp claws and teeth. They are smart, can speak, and like to solve riddles. Unicorns are powerful. They are gentle, too. They do not speak. In stories, many people hunt dragons and unicorns to show they are brave.

Mermaids look like a human and an animal combined. The top half of a mermaid is a beautiful girl. But instead of legs, she has a fish tail. Male mermaids are called mermen.

MAGICAL OBJECTS

In stories, many magical creatures carry objects that have special powers. Some magical objects heal the sick. Others make things disappear. Some humans try to steal these magical objects. This makes the owners angry. But, the magical creatures will sometimes share the magical objects if humans ask for help.

Magic wands are important magical objects in stories. Fairy godmothers use wands to grant wishes. Wizards use wands to cast spells. Some wands are made from unicorn horns. Some tales say unicorn horns can heal sick people.

It is said that some fairies have pouches of fairy dust. Just a sprinkle of it can make a person fly, disappear, or become something else. Mermaids have magical harps that can put giants to sleep.

DRAWING TIPS

You've learned about magical creatures. You're almost ready to draw them. But first, here are a few drawing tips:

Every artist needs tools. To learn how to draw magical creatures, you will need:

- Some paper
- A pencil
- An eraser
- Markers, crayons, colored pencils, or watercolors (optional)

Anyone can learn to draw. You might think only some people can draw. That's not true. Everyone can learn to draw. It takes practice, though. The more you draw, the better you will be. With practice, you will become a true artist!

Everyone makes mistakes. This is okay! Mistakes help you learn. They help you know what not to do next time. Mistakes can even make your drawing more special. It's all right if you draw an elf's ears too big. Now you've got a one-of-a-kind drawing. You can erase a mistake you don't like, too. Then start again!

Stay loose. Relax your body before you begin. Hold your pencil lightly. Don't rest your wrist on the table. Instead, move your whole arm as you draw. This will help you make smooth lines. Press lightly on the paper when you draw or erase.

Drawing is fun! The most important thing about drawing is to have fun. Be creative. Your drawings don't have to look exactly like the pictures in this book. Try changing the shape of the leprechaun's body. You can also use markers, crayons, colored pencils, or watercolors to bring your magical creatures to life.

1

2

ELF

3

4

An elf has pointy ears. It loves to play music, eat, and practice archery. Because of this, it often carries instruments and bows and arrows.

1

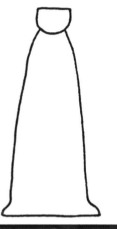

2

WIZARD

3

4

A young wizard learning his trade is called an **apprentice**. He will let his hair grow as he ages. The longer and whiter the hair is, the wiser the wizard.

1

2

MERMAID

3

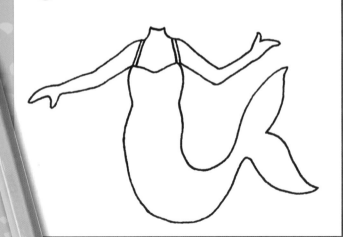

4

Mermaids have sharp fingernails and teeth for catching and eating fish. Mermaids love music. They sing a lot.

1

2

GNOME

3

4

A gnome is jolly. It lives in a home underground. It often plays tricks on human gardeners by moving a garden tool or turning on a water hose.

5

1

2

FAIRY

3

4

Many fairies have beautiful wings. Fairies can **shape-shift**.
If you frighten them, they may turn into leaves or flowers
to hide from you.

1

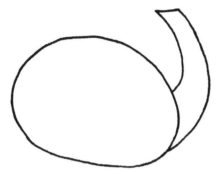

2

DRAGON

3

4

A dragon has wings and a forked tongue. It might have scales on its body, too. A dragon guards its treasure and breathes fire on anyone who tries to take it.

5

1

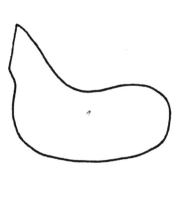

2

UNICORN

3

4

A unicorn is a beautiful, white, horse-like creature. It is best known for the horn on its head. A unicorn has **cloven hooves**. Male unicorns have beards.

1

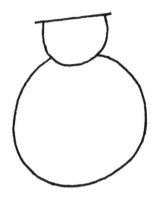

2

LEPRECHAUN

3

4

A leprechaun is small and feisty. If you catch one, he will offer you three wishes in exchange for his freedom. Leprechauns are skilled shoemakers. Their shoes have buckles, not laces.

5

MORE DRAWING

Now you know how to draw magical creatures. Here are some ways to keep drawing them.

Stories tell us that magical creatures come in all different colors, shapes, sizes, and textures. You can draw them all! Try using pens or colored pencils to draw and color in details. Experiment with crayons and markers to give your drawings different colors and textures. You can also paint your drawings. Watercolors are easy to use. If you make a mistake, you can wipe it away with a damp cloth. Try tracing the outline of your drawing with a crayon or a marker. Then paint over it with watercolor. What happens?

Drawing Using Your Imagination

When you want something new to draw, all you have to do is use your imagination! What kinds of magical creatures can you dream up? Before you start, think about your creature. Is it big or small? What color is it? Does it have wings, claws, or a tail? Does it have fur, scales, stripes, or spots? Does your creature have a magical object? Now try drawing it! If you need help, use the examples in this book to guide you.

GLOSSARY

apprentice (uh-PREN-tiss): An apprentice is someone who is learning a trade. A young wizard may be an apprentice.

cloven hooves (KLOHV-in HOOVZ): Cloven hooves have two toes instead of being smooth and round. Unicorns have cloven hooves.

folklore (FOHK-lor): Folklore is the group of customs, stories, and other traditions of a group of people. Some folklore has stories of magical creatures.

myths (MITHS): Myths are stories that try to explain beliefs or natural events. Some magical creatures come from old myths.

shape-shift (SHAYP-shift): To shape-shift means to suddenly change shape to become something else. A fairy can shape-shift.

FIND OUT MORE

BOOKS

Clibbon, Meg. *Magical Creatures*. Toronto: Annick Press, 2006.

Emberley, Ed. *Emberley's Drawing Book: Make a World*. New York: Little Brown, 2006.

Love, Carrie. *I Can Draw Magical Creatures*. New York: DK, 2006.

WEB SITES

Visit our Web site for links about drawing magical creatures:

childsworld.com/links

Note to Parents, Teachers, and Librarians: We routinely verify our Web links to make sure they are safe and active sites. So encourage your readers to check them out!

INDEX

ABOUT THE AUTHOR:
Amanda StJohn is a poet and children's book writer from Toledo, Ohio. She enjoys reading about elves and other magical creatures.

ABOUT THE ILLUSTRATOR:
For the last 25 years, Laura Ferraro Close has been illustrating children's books. She lives in Massachusetts with her husband, two sons, and dog. For her illustrations, Laura used a waterproof ink pen and watercolors that come in tubes.